NEHEMIAH

FROM RUBBLE TO REVIVAL

Materials created by Salem Alliance Church Bible Study Department
Barbara Fletcher and Sarah Bertz
Contributions by Laura Scharer and Cary Wood
Cover design by Salem Alliance Church Graphic Department
Jeff Brown
Published 2017

TABLE OF CONTENTS

LESSON #	PAGE #

PREFACE

Envision a war torn city. What do you see? I see rubble, bombed-out buildings, everything of value gone. There are no shops, no homes, no religious buildings, no roads and NO people. The heart of the city is gone.

This was Jerusalem in 586 BC. Babylon had utterly destroyed the city, killed most of its inhabitants and taken the rest captive. In essence, the city was no more. The Temple was looted and leveled, the buildings were ruined and the city walls were rubble. It was uninhabitable.

Many years later, when refugees did return, they found a city they did not recognize. In spite of the devastation—structural and emotional—they began rebuilding their lives, the city and, eventually, their Temple. Without modern day bulldozers or other kinds of equipment, their job was surely daunting and progress was painfully slow—so slow that around 90 years later, the city was still struggling to rebuild.

Even though he lived in Susa, Persia, almost a thousand miles away and worked in the King's palace,[1] word of the Jews' struggle reached an influential man named Nehemiah. He was told "Things are not going well in Jerusalem. There's great trouble and disgrace. The wall of Jerusalem has been torn down and the gates have been destroyed by fire."[2]

Nehemiah, a godly Jew, was heartbroken to hear these reports. The story of his response to that news and his calling to travel to Jerusalem and help rebuild the city is what this study is about. It is the story of a God-follower who took great risks and made great sacrifices—a wise man, a brave man, a prayer warrior and, in the end, a difference-maker. You can expect to learn from him and be inspired by him as you see how he took them from rubble to revival.

---

[1] 445 BC
[2] **Nehemiah 1:1–2**

BACKGROUND

605 BC	586 BC	539 BC	538 BC	536 BC
Babylon's first attack on Jerusalem and first partial deportation of citizens	Babylon totally destroys Jerusalem and deports all of its citizens	King Cyrus of Persia overthrows Babylon; King Cyrus implements new way of treating conquered lands	First Jewish exiles allowed to return to Jerusalem	King Cyrus sends Zerubbabel to oversee the Temple (completed between 516-515)

530 BC	522 BC	486 BC	465 BC	458 BC	445 BC
Cambyses succeeds Cyrus as King of Persia	Darius succeeds Cambyses as King of Persia	Xerxes (Esther's husband) succeeds Darius	Artaxerxes succeeds Xerxes	Artaxerxes allows Ezra to go to Jerusalem & lead religious reforms	Nehemiah travels to Jerusalem

The Babylonian Empire administered its final military blow to Israel in 586 BC.[1] Jerusalem and all of Israel were destroyed, and the citizens were either killed or marched as captives to Babylon. That remnant of Jewish people then lived in a completely pagan land hundreds of miles from their homeland. Then in 539 BC, Babylon fell to the new world power, Persia, led by King Cyrus. His political philosophy was very different from the domineering Babylonians and Assyrians. While both Babylon and Assyria had sought to destroy the countries and religions they conquered, King Cyrus wanted to rule while still respecting the various customs and beliefs of conquered people. "Convinced that sheer force could not make a large empire stable, he sought acceptance through toleration. Instead of forcing everyone to worship Persian gods, Cyrus encouraged each people group to seek its own gods' favor for him. He sent people back to their homelands, returned confiscated religious

---

[1] Babylon had first attacked Israel's Southern Kingdom (Judah) in 605 and taken many prominent hostages to Babylon, including the prophet Daniel. Thus, when the first Jews were repatriated to their homeland in 539 BC, Jeremiah's prophecy of a 70 year exile was fulfilled (**Jeremiah 29:10**).

objects and financed the rebuilding of temples. This policy was so successful that Cyrus's successors continued it (Xerxes and Artaxerxes)."[1]

The exiled Jews (so-called by themselves because they were members of the tribes of Judah, Benjamin and Levi) benefited by Cyrus' policy. He commanded the first return of the Jews to their homeland in 538 BC, and he even provided money for the expedition and the rebuilding of the Temple in Jerusalem. In addition, he restored the Temple's treasures that had been confiscated long before by the Babylonians. By 516 BC, under the combined leadership of Ezra and Zerubbabel, the Temple was rebuilt and the center of Jewish worship was re-established. Though the Temple was rebuilt, the city and its protective wall largely remained in ruins. This was the situation into which God called Nehemiah.

---

[1] *A Life Changing Encounter with God's Word from the Books of Ezra & Nehemiah.* Carol Stream, IL: NavPress, 2011. 11

RELY
LESSON 1
NEHEMIAH 1

 SET THE SCENE
Think of someone you know who is a "make it happen" person. Perhaps it is someone who planned your family reunion, re-organized your office, helped you find a new place to live or took charge of the little league team. Nehemiah was that kind of person. He was a get-it-done guy. But, on top of that, he was a devout believer in the Living God. So, when God showed him a problem, Nehemiah was totally determined to fix it, but how could a cupbearer change a whole city? He had to rely completely on God.

DIG IN

1. From **Nehemiah 1:1**, who wrote this book?[1]

    a. If you can, recall a biography or memoir you've read and what you valued about it.

    b. In AD 367, Nehemiah's biography was chosen to be part of the Canon of scripture.[2] What does that say to you about this book before you even begin?

---

[1] Tradition says that Ezra wrote 1 and 2 Chronicles, Ezra, Psalm 119 and Nehemiah. It is probable he was either Nehemiah's editor or ghost writer. Ezra and Nehemiah were one book in the Jewish Bible. *Life Application Study Bible: New Living Translation*, Carol Stream, IL: Tyndale House, 2014. 719

[2] In AD 367, the church father Athanasius first provided the complete listing of the 66 books belonging to the canon. He distinguished those from other books that were widely circulated, and he noted that those 66 books were the ones, and the only ones, universally accepted. The point is that the formation of the canon did not come all at once like a thunderbolt, but was the product of centuries of reflection and prayer. http://www.biblica.com/The International Bible Society

2. Nehemiah sets the scene in **verses 1–2**. What facts and characters do you find?[1]

   a. What did they discuss with Nehemiah? (**1:3**)

   b. What tone do you "hear" in their voices?

   c. How did Nehemiah react? (**1:4**)

 Being quick to pray was automatic for Nehemiah. Consider your own life. Is there sorrow you could stop and pray about right now?

3. Nehemiah had lived his entire life in Babylon, and yet he had a passion about his Jewish homeland and his faith.[2] Why might that be?

---

[1] By studying surviving Persian records, scholars have placed the month of Kislev as occurring within the months of November and December, 446 BC. *Life Application Study Bible: New Living Translation*, Carol Stream, IL: Tyndale House, 2014. 742

[2] A notable feature of the Persian empire was its integration of a great diversity of peoples into a single administrative system while maintaining a tradition of respect for their local customs and beliefs. The religion of the Achemenid kings was the worship of the one god Ahura-Mazda, but this was not imposed on peoples of other faiths. Rather, they were encouraged to seek the king's welfare by observing the proper forms of their own religions. Kidner, Derek. *Ezra and Nehemiah: An Introduction and Commentary.* Nottingham, England: Inter-Varsity, 2009. 20–21

a. Nehemiah was a layman,[1] not a priest or prophet. In light of that, discuss his grief over Jerusalem.

b. Below you can see an example of an ancient city wall. Now, imagine an ancient city without walls. What would the lack of walls say about that place?[2]

How would Jerusalem without walls compare to its former glory days as a great nation?

4. The first remnant of Jews had returned to Jerusalem almost 100 years earlier in 538 BC. They had rebuilt their Temple, but Jerusalem still had no walls, no protection, no stability and certainly no stature as a people-group. Read **Ezra 4:4–7; 11–23** below about the opposition they faced that led to a Persian policy initiated under King Xerxes and continued under King Artaxerxes, a policy Nehemiah would have known.

⁴ Then the local residents tried to discourage and frighten the people of Judah to keep them from their work. ⁵ They bribed agents to work against them and to frustrate their plans. This went on during the entire reign of King Cyrus of Persia and lasted until King Darius of Persia took the throne.

⁶ Years later when Xerxes began his reign, the enemies of Judah wrote a letter of accusation against the people of Judah and Jerusalem. ⁷ Even later, during the reign of King Artaxerxes of Persia, the enemies of Judah, led by Bishlam, Mithredath, and Tabeel, sent a letter to Artaxerxes in the Aramaic language, and it was translated for the king.

¹¹ This is a copy of their letter: "To King Artaxerxes, from your loyal subjects in the province west of the Euphrates River. ¹² "The king should know that the Jews who came here to Jerusalem from Babylon are rebuilding this rebellious and evil city. They have already laid the foundation and will soon finish its walls. ¹³ And the king should know that if this city is rebuilt and its walls are completed, it will be much to your disadvantage, for the Jews will then refuse to pay their tribute, customs, and tolls to you.

¹⁴ "Since we are your loyal subjects and do not want to see the king dishonored in this way, we have sent the king this information. ¹⁵ We suggest that a search be made in your ancestors' records, where you will discover what a rebellious city this has been in the past. In fact, it was destroyed because of its long and troublesome history of revolt against the kings and countries who controlled it. ¹⁶ We declare to the king that if this city is rebuilt and its walls are completed, the province west of the Euphrates River will be lost to you."

¹⁷ Then King Artaxerxes sent this reply: "To Rehum the governor, Shimshai the court secretary, and their colleagues living in Samaria and throughout the province west of the Euphrates River. Greetings. ¹⁸ "The letter you sent has been translated and read to me. ¹⁹ I ordered a search of the records and have found that Jerusalem has indeed been a hotbed of insurrection against many kings. In fact, rebellion and revolt are normal there! [20] Powerful kings have ruled over Jerusalem and the entire province west of the Euphrates River, receiving tribute, customs, and tolls. [21] Therefore, issue orders to have these men stop their work. That city must not be rebuilt except at my express command. [22] Be diligent, and don't neglect this matter, for we must not permit the situation to harm the king's interests."

[23] When this letter from King Artaxerxes was read to Rehum, Shimshai, and their colleagues, they hurried to Jerusalem. Then, with a show of strength, they forced the Jews to stop building.

a. From **Ezra 4:4–5**, what was the political goal of the local leaders?

b. How entrenched was their opposition? (**4:5–7**)

c. What did they declare to King Artaxerxes in their letter—a letter that reviewed the Persian policy established decades earlier? (**4:11–16**)

d. How did Artaxerxes respond?[1] (**4:17–23**)

5. Since Nehemiah knew about the Persian policy to thwart the rebuilding of Jerusalem, he would have been uncertain about King Artaxerxes' support.[2] Consequently, where did Nehemiah go with his heartache and concern about his people and their plight? (**Nehemiah 1:4**)

---

[1] It is apparent that Artaxerxes later changed his mind about this policy. However, you will see in succeeding lessons that the local leaders were very powerful enemies and continued to have a vested interest in not letting Judah be restored.

[2] Kidner, Derek. *Ezra and Nehemiah: An Introduction and Commentary*. Nottingham, England: Inter-Varsity, 2009. 57

a. Describe Nehemiah's intensity and your thoughts about it.

b. Read Nehemiah's prayer in **1:5–11** and note your first impressions of this layman, Nehemiah.

c. What are your initial impressions of Nehemiah's prayer?

d. Give a short heading to each section of his prayer.
   i. **1:5^1–6a**

   ii. **1:6b–7**

   iii. **1:8–10**

   iv. **1:11**

e. Why would Nehemiah list himself and his family as sinners in **verses 6–7**, when the problem being addressed hundreds of miles away was in Jerusalem?

---

^{1} The only books in the Bible that refer to God as "O Lord God of Heaven" are Ezra, Nehemiah and Daniel—all written by or about men who lived during the Babylonian exile.

f. How does **2 Chronicles 7:14** help explain why Nehemiah asked God to remember His promises?

> *Then if my people who are called by my name will humble themselves and pray and seek my face and turn from their wicked ways, I will hear from heaven and will forgive their sins and restore their land.*

 g. Are there any elements of Nehemiah's prayer that especially inspire you and make you want to incorporate them in your prayer life? If so, what?

6. Nehemiah was cupbearer to the Persian King Artaxerxes (**1:11**). What does this say to you about Nehemiah and about Artaxerxes and the Persian Empire? See the footnote below as you answer.[1]

---

[1] A cupbearer's primary responsibility was to taste the king's wine and food to assure it was not poisoned. He was often chosen for his personal attractiveness, and in ancient oriental courts was always a person of rank and importance. From the confidential nature of his duties and his frequent access to the royal presence, he possessed great influence. Unger, Merrill. *Unger's Bible Dictionary*. Chicago: Moody Press, 1959. 230

7. Nehemiah lived in pagan Persia and yet he had a passionate faith. Discuss ways to keep faith alive when the culture around you is full of different beliefs and values.

 ## RHYTHMS OF PRAYER

Nehemiah was quick to pray. Over and over again, he turned to God in the midst of the events of everyday life. Prayer was a rhythm of his life. Dialogue with God can be your rhythm of life as well.

Use these prompts to dialogue with God.

Ask God—What spiritual needs do you want me to notice around me? Are there old ruins that you want me to help rebuild?

Listen

Respond

Ask God—As you show me a problem that I can be a part of solving, what does it look like for me to rely completely on you?

Listen

Respond

PRAYER REQUESTS:

REBUILD
Lesson 2
Nehemiah 2–3

 SET THE SCENE

Most of us have been recipients of bad news at least once in our lives, so it's not hard to imagine all the emotions that follow. These can be feelings of sadness, fear, disappointment, heartache, stress, discouragement, failure or a combination of all of them. What do you do with those emotions? Do they spur you to act, to withdraw, to seek advice or to pray? Nehemiah had just received news that was very discouraging, and he immediately turned to prayer—and then to action.

DIG IN

1. Nehemiah was still reeling from the news he had received about his homeland. What did the king notice about him? (**2:1–2**)

   a. Why would it have been a big deal for Nehemiah to act this way?[1]

   b. What does this tell you about his level of grief?

   c. How did Nehemiah respond? (**2:3**)

   d. Is it your common practice to hide your grief? Why is that an automatic response?

---

[1] "The king noticed Nehemiah's sad appearance. It surprised Nehemiah to be singled out for attention and it frightened him because it was dangerous to show sorrow before the king, who could execute anyone who displeased him. In fact, anyone wearing mourning clothes was banned from the palace (**Esther 4:2**)." *Life Application Study Bible: New Living Translation*, Carol Stream, IL: Tyndale House, 2014. 744

e. How did it help Nehemiah to be vulnerable in his grief? (**2:4a**)

f. Nehemiah prayed and then responded by asking to be sent to Judah to rebuild the wall. The king granted his request. What does this exchange tell you about:

   i. Nehemiah (**2:5**)

   ii. The king (**2:6**)

   iii. Despite 90 years of oppression and long established laws forbidding the rebuilding of Jerusalem, Artaxerxes not only let Nehemiah return to build the wall, but helped him. Why would this be? (**2:7–8**)

2. Nehemiah prayed through his fear (**2:4–5**). He didn't wait until he was alone with no distractions; it was an "urgency of the moment" prayer. He needed God's wisdom, guidance and peace immediately. Have you ever had this experience? If so, share with your group.

a. Prayer is one of the most talked about actions in the New Testament. As you read through the Scriptures below, note what you learn about prayer:

   i. **Romans 8:26**

      And the Holy Spirit helps us in our weakness. For example, we don't know what God wants us to pray for. But the Holy Spirit prays for us with groanings that cannot be expressed in words.

   ii. **Romans 12:12**

      Rejoice in our confident hope. Be patient in trouble, and keep on praying.

   iii. **Ephesians 6:18**

      Pray in the Spirit at all times and on every occasion. Stay alert and be persistent in your prayers for all believers everywhere.

   iv. **Philippians 4:6–7**

      [6] Don't worry about anything; instead, pray about everything. Tell God what you need, and thank him for all he has done. [7] Then you will experience God's peace, which exceeds anything we can understand. His peace will guard your hearts and minds as you live in Christ Jesus.

   v. **1 Thessalonians 5:16–18**

      [16] Always be joyful. [17] Never stop praying. [18] Be thankful in all circumstances, for this is God's will for you who belong to Christ Jesus.

vi. **James 5:13–16**

¹³ Are any of you suffering hardships? You should pray. Are any of you happy? You should sing praises. ¹⁴ Are any of you sick? You should call for the elders of the church to come and pray over you, anointing you with oil in the name of the Lord. ¹⁵ Such a prayer offered in faith will heal the sick, and the Lord will make you well. And if you have committed any sins, you will be forgiven. ¹⁶ Confess your sins to each other and pray for each other so that you may be healed. The earnest prayer of a righteous person has great power and produces wonderful results.

b. Prayer can sometimes be hard as well as encouraging. In what ways do you want the Scriptures you just read to inspire or influence your current prayer life?

c. Pause and reflect on **Psalm 142** on the next page. Then insert concerns from your own life and pray this Psalm back to God.

¹ I cry out to the Lord; I plead for the Lord's mercy.
² I pour out my complaints before him and tell him all my troubles.
³ When I am overwhelmed, you alone know the way I should turn. Wherever I go, my enemies have set traps for me.
⁴ I look for someone to come and help me, but no one gives me a passing thought! No one will help me; no one cares a bit what happens to me.
⁵ Then I pray to you, O Lord. I say, "You are my place of refuge. You are all I really want in life.
⁶ Hear my cry, for I am very low. Rescue me from my persecutors, for they are too strong for me.
⁷ Bring me out of prison so I can thank you. The godly will crowd around me, for you are good to me."

¹ I cry out to the Lord; I plead for the Lord's mercy.

_____

_____

² I pour out my complaints before him and tell him all my troubles.

_____

_____

³ When I am overwhelmed, you alone know the way I should turn. Wherever I go, my enemies have set traps for me.
⁴ I look for someone to come and help me, but no one gives me a passing thought! No one will help me; no one cares a bit what happens to me.
⁵ Then I pray to you, O Lord. I say, "You are my place of refuge. You are all I really want in life.

_____

_____

⁶ Hear my cry, for I am very low. Rescue me from my persecutors, for they are too strong for me.

_____

_____

⁷ Bring me out of prison so I can thank you. The godly will crowd around me, for you are good to me."

_____

_____

_____

3. Nehemiah traveled to Jerusalem with many supplies and people, all granted to him by the king (**Nehemiah 2:7–10**). "There was more than protection to be gained from the military escort. It meant an arrival in style, impressively reinforcing the presentation of credentials to the neighboring governors..."[1] Imagine what this 900-mile trip on foot and horseback would have been like. How do you think they would have been received?

4. Once they arrived in Jerusalem, Nehemiah quietly began taking inventory of the situation. What did he do? (**2:11–15**)

   a. "For all his [Nehemiah's] speed and drive, he does not rush into action or into talk. He anticipates the obvious objection that a newcomer can have no idea of the task, so he briefs himself thoroughly and chooses his moment to show his hand. Above and beyond his sound tactics, however, was the conviction that basically the project was not his. It was from God and 'for Jerusalem'—not from Nehemiah nor for his prestige."[2] Does this quote provide any new insights about Nehemiah? If so, what?

---

[1] Kidner, Derek. *Ezra and Nehemiah: An Introduction and Commentary*. Nottingham, England: Inter-Varsity, 2009. 88
[2] Ibid 89

b. As you think over **Nehemiah 2:13–14**, look at this map.[1] What interests you about the areas that Nehemiah surveyed?

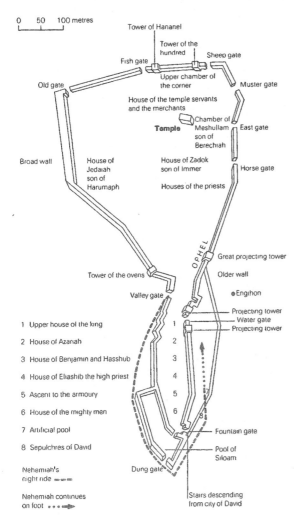

0   50   100 metres

Tower of Hananel

Tower of the hundred

Sheep gate

Fish gate

Upper chamber of the corner

Muster gate

Old gate

House of the temple servants and the merchants

Temple

Chamber of Meshullam son of Berechiah

East gate

Broad wall

House of Jedaiah son of Harumaph

House of Zadok son of Immer

Houses of the priests

Horse gate

OPHEL

Great projecting tower

Tower of the ovens

Older wall

Valley gate

Engihon

1 Upper house of the king

Projecting tower
Water gate
Projecting tower

2 House of Azariah

3 House of Benjamin and Hasshub

4 House of Eliashib the high priest

5 Ascent to the armoury

6 House of the mighty men

7 Artificial pool

Fountain gate

8 Sepulchres of David

Pool of Siloam

Nehemiah's night ride ▬ ▬ ▬

Dung gate

Nehemiah continues on foot ▪ ▪ ▪ ▬►

Stairs descending from city of David

c. If you were Nehemiah, how would you have been feeling about the task ahead?

---

[1] Kidner, Derek. *Ezra and Nehemiah: An Introduction and Commentary*. Nottingham, England: Inter-Varsity, 2009. 93

d. How did the officials first respond to him? (**2:16–18**)

e. Who opposed Nehemiah, and how did Nehemiah respond to them? (**2:19–20**)

f. What do you think about his boldness and confidence?

5. Chapter three is filled with the names of those who helped Nehemiah rebuild the wall and where they worked. Read through the chapter and note a few people that stand out to you.

a. What intrigues you about these people?

b. Why do you think Nehemiah went into such detail to tell readers who rebuilt the wall and where?

c. In order to record all these names and professions, Nehemiah had to learn them. Consider this fact and comment on what that revealed about Nehemiah as a leader.

 RHYTHMS OF PRAYER

Nehemiah was quick to pray. Over and over again, he was quick to turn to God in the midst of the events of his everyday life. Prayer was a rhythm of life for Nehemiah. Dialogue with God can be our rhythm of life as well.

Use these prompts to dialogue with God.

Ask God—Is there a recent difficult situation that you would encourage me bring to you in prayer?

Listen

Respond

Ask God—What do you want to say to me about this situation? How do you respond to my emotions of sadness, fear, disappointment, heartache, stress, discouragement, failure, etc.?

Listen

Respond

Ask God—Is there an action that you would guide me to take in this situation?

Listen

Respond

PRAYER REQUESTS:

REJECTION
LESSON 3
NEHEMIAH 4

 SET THE SCENE
Have you ever been involved with something that was off to a great start but then problems arose? Maybe you even experienced opposition. Perhaps you easily sold your home, but then the inspection revealed problems you have to fix. Or, you excitedly took a new job and then discovered it wasn't what you expected and the people you work with were difficult. Such was the case for Nehemiah. He was off to a strong start with support from King Artaxerxes and the Jewish leaders in Jerusalem. They were "all in" for rebuilding the wall, and they started with a bang, but then serious opposition and rejection arose from very difficult and determined people.

DIG IN

1. Who opposed the Jews and how would you describe his attitude? **(4:1–2)**

    a. Sanballat was the governor of Samaria,[1] the area just north of Jerusalem and Judah. Discuss his potential power and influence as an opponent.

    b. Opposition from the Persian Empire toward Judah wasn't new. It had started decades earlier. Review Lesson 1, question 4 regarding **Ezra 4:6–23**. Describe the decree enacted back then.

---

[1] *Life Application Study Bible: New Living Translation*, Carol Stream, IL: Tyndale House, 2014. 748

c. Who did Sanballat immediately involve in his opposition? (**4:2–3**)

d. This was not Sanballat's first rejection of Jewish rebuilding efforts.[1] Furthermore, according to ancient Persian documents, Nehemiah's opponents were men of considerable status. Not only was Sanballat the governor of Samaria,[2] Geshem was the leader of a powerful group of Arab communities, and Tobiah was probably governor of Ammon as well as a member of an influential Jewish family.

How would you react if such people opposed and ridiculed a project that was as important to you as the wall was to Nehemiah?

 e. How did Nehemiah react? (**4:4–5**)

---

[1] See **Nehemiah 2:19**: "When Sanballat, Tobiah, and Geshem the Arab heard of our plan, they scoffed contemptuously. 'What are you doing? Are you rebelling against the king?' they asked."

[2] When the Northern Kingdom of Israel was destroyed in 722 BC by the Assyrians, the Assyrians re-settled many pagans in the land (**2 Kings 17:24–41**). After that, the religion of the area turned into Judaism with paganism thrown in. For centuries thereafter, Jews who practiced a pure Judaism hated Samaritans. This is evident in the Gospels. "The woman [at the well] was surprised, for Jews refuse to have anything to do with Samaritans. "She said to Jesus, 'You are a Jew, and I am a Samaritan woman. Why are you asking me for a drink?'" (**John 4:9**) It seems Sanballat was a Jew in name only, or perhaps he practiced a mixed religion of Judaism and paganism like most Samarians.

i. Discuss your thoughts about Nehemiah's prayer in **Nehemiah 4:5**.

ii. What do you do with your emotions when facing serious rejection or opposition?

iii. How could you pray them to God?

f. Where were Sanballat, his friends and military officers when they declared their rejection of the wall building project, according to the end of **verse 5**?

How might this have impacted the whole situation?

2. Nonetheless, what did Nehemiah and his workers do next? (**4:6**)

How does ridicule affect you? Does it motivate or discourage you?

3. **Nehemiah 4:7–8** reveals an escalation of the opposition and rejection. What was it?[1]

 How did Nehemiah and his workers handle it? (**4:9**)

4. The people of Judah spoke up and expressed their thoughts to Nehemiah. What did they say? (**4:10–12**)

    a. Are you surprised by their fear or discouragement? Why or why not?

---

[1] With the Ashdodites now added to the opposition, the enemy alliance included the Ashdodites and Samarians from the north, Tobiah and the Ammonites from the east, and the Arabs from the south. In other words, it was extensive. Kidner, Derek. *Ezra and Nehemiah: An Introduction and Commentary.* Nottingham, England: Inter-Varsity, 2009. 99

b. What action did Nehemiah take, and how did he motivate his workers? (**4:13–14**)

c. If you were on Nehemiah's work crew, how might Nehemiah's strategy and speech change your attitude?

5. What servant leadership qualities do you see in Nehemiah based on his words and actions so far in this chapter? Don't forget that Nehemiah was not a priest or prophet, but simply a faithful God-follower.

a. List the various ways the Jews protected themselves and the ways Nehemiah helped relieve their anxiety. (**4:15–20**)

b. What reason for the failure of the opposition's plot did Nehemiah give in **4:15**?

c. What additional protections do you discover in **4:21–23**?

d. Would you want to work under a leader like Nehemiah? Why or why not?

6. How has Nehemiah 4 inspired you about doing life while facing rejection, opposition or difficulties?

 ## RHYTHMS OF PRAYER

Nehemiah was quick to pray. Over and over again, he was quick to turn to God in the midst of the events of his everyday life. Prayer was a rhythm of life for Nehemiah. Dialogue with God can be our rhythm of life as well.

Use these prompts to dialogue with God.

Ask God—Is there a recent experience of rejection, opposition, ridicule or difficulty that you would want me to bring to you in prayer?

Listen

Respond

Ask God—How do you want to show me that you are my defender and that you will fight for me?

Listen

Respond

PRAYER REQUESTS:

RECTIFY
LESSON 4
NEHEMIAH 5

 SET THE SCENE
Can you imagine being in such a desperate place that you were forced to sell your child into child-labor in order to afford to feed the rest of your family? And what if the person buying your child were not a stranger, but a distant relative? In chapter five the Jews rebuilding the wall faced hardship caused by their own people. When they were at the end of their rope and struggling for survival, their own families took advantage of them and their children. Nehemiah was appalled and did what he could to rectify the situation.

DIG IN

1. What were the Jewish men and their wives saying? (**Nehemiah 5:1–4**)

   a. Describe the heartache in **Nehemiah 5:5**.

   b. Climb into their reality. How would you feel if you were working all day and couldn't find a way to feed your family?

2. List the various elements of Nehemiah's response to their complaints. (5:6–8)

a. Read **Exodus 22:25–26** and **Leviticus 25:35–37**. Ponder their relevance to this situation.

   i. **Exodus 22:25–26**

   25 If you lend money to any of my people who are in need, do not charge interest as a money lender would. 26 If you take your neighbor's cloak as security for a loan, you must return it before sunset.

   ii. **Leviticus 25:35–37**

   35 If one of your fellow Israelites falls into poverty and cannot support himself, support him as you would a foreigner or a temporary resident and allow him to live with you. 36 Do not charge interest or make a profit at his expense. Instead, show your fear of God by letting him live with you as your relative. 37 Remember, do not charge interest on money you lend him or make a profit on food you sell him.

   iii. How do the verses above help explain Nehemiah's anger?

b. Do you see the principles of **James 1:19** in Nehemiah's response? How?

Understand this, my dear brothers and sisters: You must all be quick to listen, slow to speak, and slow to get angry.

    i. How do you respond when you are angry?

    ii. What causes you to speak out? What causes you to keep quiet?

    iii. What might God be saying to you about managing anger?

3. How did Nehemiah ask the nobles and officials to right the situation? (**Nehemiah 5:9–11**)

    a. Read and react to their response in **verse 12a**.

    b. How did Nehemiah guarantee this promise? (**5:12b–13**)

4. How did Nehemiah and his officials act differently than the governors before them?
   a. **Verse 14**

   b. **Verse 15**

   c. **Verse 16**

   d. **Verse 17**

   e. **Verse 18**

   f. How do Nehemiah's actions live out the most important commandments found in **Mark 12:28–31**?

   28 One of the teachers of religious law was standing there listening to the debate. He realized that Jesus had answered well, so he asked, "Of all the commandments, which is the most important?" 29 Jesus replied, "The most important commandment is this: 'Listen, O Israel! The LORD our God is the one and only LORD. 30 And you must love the LORD our God with all your heart, all your soul, all your mind, and all your strength.' 31 The second is equally important: 'Love your neighbor as yourself.' No other commandment is greater than these."

g. Has God called you to sacrifice any personal rights, like Nehemiah did, in order to live out the gospel? If so, what?[1] Take time to process this with God. Share with your group if you feel comfortable.

5. If you were to describe Nehemiah to a friend right now, what would you say?

RHYTHMS OF PRAYER

Nehemiah was quick to pray. Over and over again, he was quick to turn to God in the midst of the events of his everyday life. Prayer was a rhythm of life for Nehemiah. Dialogue with God can be our rhythm of life as well.

Use these prompts to dialogue with God.

God, I am appalled and angry about _____

_____

_____

_____

I see Your glory and Your name being hurt.

---

[1] *A Life Changing Encounter with God's Word from the Books of Ezra & Nehemiah*. Carol Stream, IL: NavPress, 2011. 62

Ask God—How would you like me to respond? To handle my anger?

Listen

Respond

Ask God—Are you calling me to sacrifice any personal rights in order to live out the gospel?

Listen

Respond

PRAYER REQUESTS:

LESSON 5
NEHEMIAH 6–7

 SET THE SCENE
Attacked, trapped, plotted against, harassed and bullied are
all negative words and things you hope never happen to you or those
you love. All of those things happened to Nehemiah and the people
of Jerusalem as they were attempting to do what some considered
impossible. They had been oppressed by outsiders and even by their own
people. Despite all of that, they were accomplishing what God had called
them to do, thanks to God's power and Nehemiah's leadership. Even
though they could see the light at the end of the tunnel, the opposition
was far from over.

 DIG IN

1. The Jews had finished rebuilding the walls. Only the gates were yet to
   be finished. Nehemiah's enemies—Sanballat, Tobiah and Geshem—
   asked to meet with him. How did Nehemiah respond and why? **(6:1–3)**

   a. This happened four times. What happened on the fifth time and
      how did Nehemiah react? **(6:4–8)**

   b. "The fact that Sanballat had an open, or unsealed, letter delivered
      to Nehemiah shows that he wanted to make sure the letter's
      content was made public."[1] Why do you think Sanballat did this?
      What effect do you think this would have had?

---

[1] *Life Application Study Bible: New Living Translation*, Carol Stream, IL: Tyndale House,
2014. 752

Today, open letters are often seen in our news feeds on social media and in newspapers. They are opinions; some are based in truth, some are not. Have you read one? Written one? Does this change the way you view Sanballat's letter? If so, how?

   c. What was the purpose of these messages? Ultimately, what did they accomplish? (**6:9**)

2. These men continued their attack on Nehemiah. Read **6:10–14** and note what they tried to do.

   a. In **verse 14**, prayer is—again—the thing that Nehemiah turned to in hard times. This reinforces the value Nehemiah placed on his relationship with the Lord. This time it was because his reputation was at stake. Compare Nehemiah's reaction to David's in **Psalm 3:1–8** below.

    ¹ O LORD, I have so many enemies;
      so many are against me.
    ² So many are saying,
      "God will never rescue him!"
    ³ But you, O LORD, are a shield around me;
      you are my glory, the one who holds my head high.
    ⁴ I cried out to the LORD,
      and he answered me from his holy mountain.
    ⁵ I lay down and slept,
      yet I woke up in safety,
      for the LORD was watching over me.
    ⁶ I am not afraid of ten thousand enemies
      who surround me on every side.

7 Arise, O LORD!
Rescue me, my God!
Slap all my enemies in the face!
Shatter the teeth of the wicked!
8 Victory comes from you, O LORD.
May you bless your people.

b. When you are being intimidated or falsely accused, how do you react?

c. Read **Nehemiah 6:15–16** and describe the amazing feat recorded there despite opposition.

3. Even in the victory and excitement of completing the wall, Nehemiah faced ridicule, opposition, taunts and threats (**6:17–19**). Still, Nehemiah seemed to handle himself well during this time. From **7:1–3**, how did Nehemiah go about protecting himself and the people?

4. What idea did God give Nehemiah in **7:5**? Why? **(7:4)**

a. Why do you think Nehemiah was able to so readily hear ideas from God?

b. Has God ever given you ideas? What has that looked like?

c. How could you grow this part of your relationship with God? Brainstorm with your group.

5. Quickly read through the list of families in **7:6–73**. Why do you think this list was important?[1]

a. Why were some people disqualified from serving? **(7:63–65)**

---

[1] Genealogies were greatly valued because it was vitally important for a Jew to be able to prove that he or she was a descendant of Abraham and was, therefore, part of God's people. *Life Application Study Bible: New Living Translation*, Carol Stream, IL: Tyndale House, 2014. 755

b. Do you think this was fair? Why or why not?

c. As followers of Christ, our names are written in God's Book of Life (**Philippians 4:3**), and our names will never be erased (**Revelations 3:5**). What does this truth mean to you?

 RHYTHMS OF PRAYER

Nehemiah was quick to pray. Over and over again, he was quick to turn to God in the midst of the events of his everyday life. Prayer was a rhythm of life for Nehemiah. Dialogue with God can be our rhythm of life as well.

Use these prompts to dialogue with God.

Ask God—What is the work you have called me to, despite opposition?

Listen

Respond like Nehemiah—"Now strengthen my hands" (**6:9**)

PRAYER REQUESTS:

REVIVAL
LESSON 6
NEHEMIAH 8–9

 SET THE SCENE

Think of your wedding or a friend's wedding. Weddings are beautiful events which take a long time and much effort to plan. Finally the day comes; it's wonderful, and you think, "Yay, we did it!" However, you soon realize there's a home to be created, a relationship to deepen, a marriage to build and many hurdles to climb together in life. So it was for Nehemiah and Jerusalem.

The wall was finished! It was a phenomenal accomplishment in just two months and definitely cause for great celebration. Nehemiah could have headed home to Susa and his job with King Artaxerxes with a sense of accomplishment. However, as he surveyed the people, he realized his job wasn't over. The Israelites weren't in a good place spiritually, and they knew it. They needed revival.

 DIG IN

1. After they had settled in their towns, where did the Israelites[1] gather, and what did they request? (**8:1**)

    a. How is the document described at the end of **verse 1**?

    b. Who gathered to hear it? What do you observe about them? (**8:1–3**)

---
[1] The text switches from calling them the Jews to calling them the Israelites, therefore, we changed as well.

c. Who read the Law, and what do you learn about him in **Ezra 7:1–26**? Underline your observations.

7:1 *Many years later, during the reign of King Artaxerxes of Persia, there was a man named Ezra. He was the son of Seraiah, son of Azariah, son of Hilkiah,* 2 *son of Shallum, son of Zadok, son of Ahitub,* 3 *son of Amariah, son of Azariah, son of Meraioth,* 4 *son of Zerahiah, son of Uzzi, son of Bukki,* 5 *son of Abishua, son of Phinehas, son of Eleazar, son of Aaron the high priest.* 6 *This Ezra was a scribe who was well versed in the Law of Moses, which the Lord, the God of Israel, had given to the people of Israel. He came up to Jerusalem from Babylon, and the king gave him everything he asked for, because the gracious hand of the Lord his God was on him.* 7 *Some of the people of Israel, as well as some of the priests, Levites, singers, gatekeepers, and Temple servants, traveled up to Jerusalem with him in the seventh year of King Artaxerxes' reign.*

8 *Ezra arrived in Jerusalem in August of that year.* 9 *He had arranged to leave Babylon on April 8, the first day of the new year, and he arrived at Jerusalem on August 4, for the gracious hand of his God was on him.* 10 *This was because Ezra had determined to study and obey the Law of the Lord and to teach those decrees and regulations to the people of Israel.*

11 *King Artaxerxes had given a copy of the following letter to Ezra, the priest and scribe who studied and taught the commands and decrees of the Lord to Israel:* 12 *"From Artaxerxes, the king of kings, to Ezra the priest, the teacher of the law of the God of heaven. Greetings.*

13 *"I decree that any of the people of Israel in my kingdom, including the priests and Levites, may volunteer to return to Jerusalem with you.* 14 *I and my council of seven hereby instruct you to conduct an inquiry into the situation in Judah and Jerusalem, based on your God's law, which is in your hand.* 15 *We also commission you to take with you silver and gold, which we are freely presenting as an offering to the God of Israel who lives in Jerusalem.*

16 *"Furthermore, you are to take any silver and gold that you may obtain from the province of Babylon, as well as the voluntary offerings of the people and the priests that are presented for the Temple of their God in Jerusalem.* 17 *These donations are to be used specifically for the purchase of bulls, rams, male lambs, and the appropriate grain offerings and liquid offerings, all of which will be offered on the altar of the Temple of your God in Jerusalem.*

18 Any silver and gold that is left over may be used in whatever way you and your colleagues feel is the will of your God. *19* "But as for the cups we are entrusting to you for the service of the Temple of your God, deliver them all to the God of Jerusalem. *20* If you need anything else for your God's Temple or for any similar needs, you may take it from the royal treasury.

21 "I, Artaxerxes the king, hereby send this decree to all the treasurers in the province west of the Euphrates River: 'You are to give Ezra, the priest and teacher of the law of the God of heaven, whatever he requests of you. *22* You are to give him up to 7,500 pounds of silver, 500 bushels of wheat, 550 gallons of wine, 550 gallons of olive oil, and an unlimited supply of salt. *23* Be careful to provide whatever the God of heaven demands for his Temple, for why should we risk bringing God's anger against the realm of the king and his sons? *24* I also decree that no priest, Levite, singer, gatekeeper, Temple servant, or other worker in this Temple of God will be required to pay tribute, customs, or tolls of any kind.'

25 "And you, Ezra, are to use the wisdom your God has given you to appoint magistrates and judges who know your God's laws to govern all the people in the province west of the Euphrates River. Teach the law to anyone who does not know it. *26* Anyone who refuses to obey the law of your God and the law of the king will be punished immediately, either by death, banishment, confiscation of goods, or imprisonment."

Summarize your impressions of Ezra.

2. As Ezra stood before them, what were their postures? (Nehemiah 8:4–6)

    a. How do their various postures speak to you of their hearts toward God and His Word?

    b. Typically, what is your posture before God and why?

    c. What role do you think Nehemiah's leadership played in their eager hearts toward God?

3. What was the Israelites' response to hearing and learning (gaining insight) from the Law? (Nehemiah 8:9)

    a. Why do you think they had this response?

    b. Have you ever had this response when you've felt far from God? What was it like?

c. Why would Nehemiah (now the governor) say that celebration was a better reaction for them than grief? (**9–10**)

d. Notice they celebrated when they heard God's Words and understood them. (**11–12**) Have you ever experienced this?

e. Read **Luke 15:11–32**. How and why does this story illustrate the joy of the Lord?

f. How can the joy of the Lord be our strength?

4. The gathering continued. The family leaders and priests kept studying the Law, and they learned there was a festival that was supposed to happen that month. What were the people told to do, and how did they respond? (**Nehemiah 8:13–17**)[1]

---

[1] "During the seven-day Festival of Shelters, the people lived in shelters made of branches. This practice was instituted as a reminder of their rescue from Egypt and the time spent in shelters in the wilderness. They were to think about God's protection and guidance during their years of wandering and the fact that God would still protect and guide them if they obeyed Him. This was a time to remember their origins." *Life Application Study Bible: New Living Translation*, Carol Stream, IL: Tyndale House, 2014. 756. See **Leviticus 23:43**.

a. What parallels can you find between the purpose of the Festival of Shelters and the Israelites' return from Babylon?

b. What did Ezra do for the people? (**Nehemiah 8:18**)

c. What value do you see in an eight-day religious celebration?

5. The feast ended on October 22, and nine days later the Israelites gathered again. They dressed in burlap, sprinkled themselves with dust and confessed their sins (**9:1–2**). What did burlap and dust represent, according to the verses below?

A man from the tribe of Benjamin ran from the battlefield and arrived at Shiloh later that same day. He had torn his clothes and put dust on his head to show his grief. (**1 Samuel 4:12**)

⁶ When the king of Nineveh heard what Jonah was saying, he stepped down from his throne and took off his royal robes. He dressed himself in burlap and sat on a heap of ashes. ⁷ Then the king and his nobles sent this decree throughout the city: "No one, not even the animals from your herds and flocks, may eat or drink anything at all. ⁸ People and animals alike must wear garments of mourning, and everyone must pray earnestly to God. They must turn from their evil ways and stop all their violence. (**Jonah 3:6–8**)

a. What happened in **Nehemiah 9:3–4**?

b. How teachable are you as you sit under the Scriptures?

    i. How teachable do you want to be?

    ii. Pause and talk to God about this.

6. How did the Levitical leaders continue the worship service? (**9:5**)

 a. Read through the prayer in **9:6–37**. Summarize a few parts of Israel's history as found in this prayer.

b. Remember that the Israelites didn't have Bibles, so this prayer was a way to rehearse and learn their history. Give at least two other reasons to pray this way.

c. Read **Psalm 107:43**.[1] Take a few minutes to list ways God has provided in your history and pray them back as praise to God.

 RHYTHMS OF PRAYER

Nehemiah was quick to pray. Over and over again, he was quick to turn to God in the midst of the events of his everyday life. Prayer was a rhythm of life for Nehemiah. Dialogue with God can be our rhythm of life as well.

Use these prompts to dialogue with God.

Ask God—How can I celebrate the work you have done in my life, my family, my community?

Listen

Respond

God, as a part of my worship, I bring my confessions before you:

Ask God—As I listen to your Word, is there a work of revival that you want to do in my life, my family, community?

Listen

Respond

---

[1] It was written after the psalmist rehearsed God's faithfulness throughout Israel's history.

PRAYER REQUESTS:

RECOMMITMENT
LESSON 7
NEHEMIAH 10–11

 SET THE SCENE

To make a promise is a big deal. Unfortunately, the value of a promise is quickly decreasing because of the flippant and casual way our culture uses the word. We make pinky promises as kids and don't follow through; we promise to do something for a friend or loved one but run out of time or motivation; we promise to love and cherish a spouse yet divorce rates keep rising. Rarely do people count the cost of a promise before they make one.

A promise should not be made lightly. It is a serious commitment, bond and vow. Too often people are hurt by broken promises. Even if the consequences seem small, the lasting ramifications of a broken promise can be huge—hurt feelings, broken relationships, lost trust—just to name a few.

The Jewish people were making a promise to God to recommit themselves to Him. This was no small decision, but a life-changing one that was meant to affect every aspect of their daily lives.

DIG IN

1. The people had just had a spiritual revival. They repented and confessed their sins to God. How did they seal their promise? **(9:38–10:27)**

   a. What groups of people were involved?

   b. Why do you think it was important for these groups to ratify it?

2. Read **10:28–29** and make several observations about what happened next.

3. Read through the commitment/vow the people made to the Lord. Underline each promise they made.

   30 "We promise not to let our daughters marry the pagan people of the land, and not to let our sons marry their daughters. 31 "We also promise that if the people of the land should bring any merchandise or grain to be sold on the Sabbath or on any other holy day, we will refuse to buy it. Every seventh year we will let our land rest, and we will cancel all debts owed to us. 32 "In addition, we promise to obey the command to pay the annual Temple tax of one-eighth of an ounce of silver for the care of the Temple of our God. 33 This will provide for the Bread of the Presence; for the regular grain offerings and burnt offerings; for the offerings on the Sabbaths, the new moon celebrations, and the annual festivals; for the holy offerings; and for the sin offerings to make atonement for Israel. It will provide for everything necessary for the work of the Temple of our God. 34 "We have cast sacred lots to determine when—at regular times each year—the families of the priests, Levites, and the common people should bring wood to God's Temple to be burned on the altar of the Lord our God, as is written in the Law. 35 "We promise to bring the first part of every harvest to the Lord's Temple year after year—whether it be a crop from the soil or from our fruit trees. 36 We agree to give God our oldest sons and the firstborn of all our herds and flocks, as prescribed in the Law. We will present them to the priests who minister in the Temple of our God. 37 We will store the produce in the storerooms of the Temple of our God. We will bring the best of our flour and other grain offerings, the best of our fruit, and the best of our new wine and olive oil. And we promise to bring to the Levites a tenth of everything our land produces, for it is the Levites who collect the tithes in all our rural towns. 38 "A priest—a descendant of Aaron— will be with the Levites as they receive these tithes. And a tenth of all that is collected as tithes will be delivered by the Levites to the Temple of our God and placed in the storerooms. 39 The people and the Levites must bring these offerings of grain, new wine, and olive oil to the storerooms and place them in the sacred containers near the ministering priests, the gatekeepers, and the singers. "We promise together not to neglect the Temple of our God."

    a. Note several promises you find interesting and discuss them with your group.

    b. These were specific promises the Israelites decided to make to the Lord.

       i. What are some underlying principles that still apply today?

       ii. Which ones resonate with you personally? How is God asking you to live them out?

4. Merriam-Webster defines a vow as "a serious promise to do something or to behave in a certain way." How would you define it?

    a. How seriously do you take making a vow/promise?

b. What are some of the consequences you have seen as a result of broken promises?

5. What do the following Scriptures tell you about God as a Promise-keeper? Note how they impact you.
   a. **Psalm 145:13**

   For your kingdom is an everlasting kingdom.
   You rule throughout all generations.
   The Lord always keeps his promises;
   he is gracious in all he does.

   b. **Psalm 146:6**

   He made heaven and earth,
   the sea, and everything in them.
   He keeps every promise forever.

   c. **Hebrews 6:17–18**

   [17] God also bound himself with an oath, so that those who received the promise could be perfectly sure that he would never change his mind. [18] So God has given both his promise and his oath. These two things are unchangeable because it is impossible for God to lie. Therefore, we who have fled to him for refuge can have great confidence as we hold to the hope that lies before us.

d. **Hebrews 10:23**

   Let us hold tightly without wavering to the hope we affirm, for God can be trusted to keep his promise.

e. What would your life be like if God were not a promise-keeper?

6. After the Israelites recommitted themselves to God, Nehemiah addressed another concern: who would live inside the Jerusalem walls. Consider the following quote about this:

   "The exiles who returned were few in number compared to Jerusalem's population in the days of the kings. And because the walls had been rebuilt on their original foundations, the city seemed sparsely populated. Nehemiah asked one-tenth of the people from the outlying areas to move inside the city walls to keep large areas of the city from being vacant. Apparently these people did not want to move into the city. Only a few people volunteered (**11:1–2**), and Nehemiah determined by sacred lot who among the remaining people would have to move. Many of them may not have wanted to live in the city because (1) non-Jews attached a stigma to Jerusalem residents, often excluding them from trade because of their religious beliefs; (2) moving into the city meant rebuilding their homes and reestablishing their businesses, a major investment of time and money; (3) living in Jerusalem required stricter obedience to God's Word because of greater social pressure and proximity to the Temple."[1]

   a. Would you have wanted to live in Jerusalem? Why or why not?

---

[1] *Life Application Study Bible: New Living Translation*, Carol Stream, IL: Tyndale House, 2014. 761

b. What do you think of Nehemiah's choice to cast lots to make a decision?

c. Are there things you have been asked to do in the last year that are hard or uncomfortable? What was the result? Share your experience with your group.

 RHYTHMS OF PRAYER

Nehemiah was quick to pray. Over and over again, he was quick to turn to God in the midst of the events of his everyday life. Prayer was a rhythm of life for Nehemiah. Dialogue with God can be our rhythm of life as well.

Use these prompts to dialogue with God.

Ask God—What promises have I made to you that I have broken?

Listen

Respond

Ask God—Is there a particular recommitment or promise that you are asking me to make?

Listen

Respond

Ask God—What kinds of changes do I need to make in order to keep this promise?

Listen

Respond

PRAYER REQUESTS:

REFORM
LESSON 8
NEHEMIAH 12–13

 SET THE SCENE

It's an age-old story. Someone decides to change a habit, go on a diet, stop drinking or adjust a behavior; almost as soon as the decision is made, the old patterns resurface. Changing a life pattern doesn't happen overnight. It's not easy, and it can't be done without God and supportive people. It involves a total mind and heart shift. Certainly that would be true for the Jews. Would they be able to do it?

 DIG IN

1. Picture your family tree or the family tree of a famous family or monarch. Most likely it will look something like this:[1]

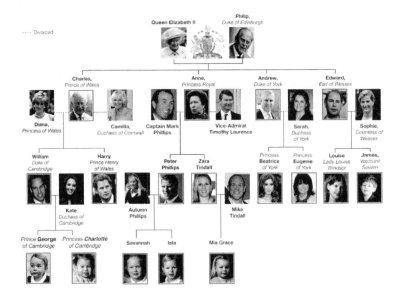

In the Bible, family trees look a little different. Typically, they are just lists of names, yet they were extremely important for the Israelites to know. The list in **Nehemiah 12:1–26**, covers multiple spiritual family trees from approximately 538 BC–430 BC.

---

[1] Taken from bbc.com

Why do you think only the leaders were mentioned?

2. After listing the spiritual leaders, Nehemiah and the people of Israel had a celebration to rededicate the walls of Jerusalem to God. Read through the description of the celebration in **Nehemiah 12:27–47**. Why would they dedicate the wall to God? What do you think was the significance of this action?

    a. Imagine being there. How would you describe this scene?

    b. How does this celebration compare to how we celebrate God's work among us today, both individually and corporately?

    c. How does David's worship in **Psalms 149:1–5** and **150:1–6** compare with the celebration in Nehemiah?
        ¹ Praise the LORD!
        Sing to the LORD a new song.
        *   Sing his praises in the assembly of the faithful.*
        ² O Israel, rejoice in your Maker.
        *   O people of Jerusalem, exult in your King.*
        ³ Praise his name with dancing,
        *   accompanied by tambourine and harp.*
        ⁴ For the LORD delights in his people;
        *   he crowns the humble with victory.*

⁵ Let the faithful rejoice that he honors them.
Let them sing for joy as they lie on their beds.

¹ Praise the LORD!
Praise God in his sanctuary;
praise him in his mighty heaven!
² Praise him for his mighty works;
praise his unequaled greatness!
³ Praise him with a blast of the ram's horn;
praise him with the lyre and harp!
⁴ Praise him with the tambourine and dancing;
praise him with strings and flutes!
⁵ Praise him with a clash of cymbals;
praise him with loud clanging cymbals.
⁶ Let everything that breathes sing praises to the LORD!
Praise the LORD!

   i. What seems similar? What seems different?

   ii. How does/can this influence your current view of, and participation in, worship?

3. Nehemiah returned to Babylon after 12 years in Jerusalem. What happened once he left? (**Nehemiah 13:1–5**)

a. Why was Tobiah given a room in the Temple? (**13:4–5**) Why do you think this was a big deal?

b. Nehemiah returned to Jerusalem. What was one of the first things he did? Why? (**13:6–9**)

c. Read **Matthew 21:12–13** about Jesus and how He reacted to misuse of the temple. Note the similarities.

12 Jesus entered the Temple and began to drive out all the people buying and selling animals for sacrifice. He knocked over the tables of the money changers and the chairs of those selling doves. 13 He said to them, "The Scriptures declare, 'My Temple will be called a house of prayer,' but you have turned it into a den of thieves!"

d. Why would both Jesus and Nehemiah have such strong reactions?

e. What does this say to you about Nehemiah?

f. Do you think Nehemiah reacted wisely or rashly? Did he overreact? Why or why not?

4. In **Nehemiah 13:10**, what else did Nehemiah discover?

   a. How did Nehemiah respond? **(13:11–13)**

   b. Nehemiah prayed after he did these things. Think of a time you did something for God and complete this prayer. **(Nehemiah 13:14)**

Remember this _____

_____

_____

O my God, and do not forget all that I have faithfully done _____

_____

_____

Discuss with you group how it made you feel to pray this way.

   c. When Nehemiah was in Jerusalem, the people remained faithful. Accountability is a huge piece of faithfulness. What areas in your life tend to slip when there is a lack of accountability? It could be finances, diet, thoughts, spiritual practices, etc. Think of someone you could invite to encourage you in these areas.

5. Nehemiah called for the people to reform and return to their commitment to God. What were they doing on the Sabbath? (**13:15–16**)

a. In **13:17–18**, Nehemiah declared they were desecrating the Sabbath. Why would this be so terrible? Keep **Exodus 20:8–11** in mind as you answer.

   8 "Remember to observe the Sabbath day by keeping it holy.
   9 You have six days each week for your ordinary work, 10 but the seventh day is a Sabbath day of rest dedicated to the Lord your God. On that day no one in your household may do any work. This includes you, your sons and daughters, your male and female servants, your livestock, and any foreigners living among you.
   11 For in six days the Lord made the heavens, the earth, the sea, and everything in them; but on the seventh day he rested. That is why the Lord blessed the Sabbath day and set it apart as holy.

b. What does it look like to honor the Sabbath in your life?

c. How does **Isaiah 58:13** further reveal God's heart about the Sabbath?

d. What Sabbath reforms did Nehemiah institute in **Nehemiah 13:19–22**?

6. Nehemiah also addressed marriage to non-Jewish foreigners. What dramatic actions did he take? (13:23–30)

    a. What do you think of his actions?

    b. Why did he react this way? (24, 26–27)

7. Read Nehemiah's prayers in 13:14, 22, 29, 31. Comment on his interaction with God.

Based on your study of Nehemiah, summarize your thoughts of Nehemiah as a man of prayer.

RHYTHMS OF PRAYER

Nehemiah was quick to pray. Over and over again, he was quick to turn to God in the midst of the events of his everyday life. Prayer was a rhythm of life for Nehemiah. Dialogue with God can be our rhythm of life as well.

Use these prompts to dialogue with God.

God—I've rededicated myself to you.

Humbly praise God once again for ways He has worked in your life. List at least four as you bow your head and heart before Him. Write your words of worship and praise here:

Ask God—As I strive to be faithful to the promises I have made to you and others, I confess I need your help. As old patterns resurface, please stop me in my tracks. Gracious God, heal my weakneses:_____
_____
_____

Transform me Jesus!

Listen

Respond

PRAYER REQUESTS: